Collins

Revised Edition

Vision 2

A Course on Values and Life Skills

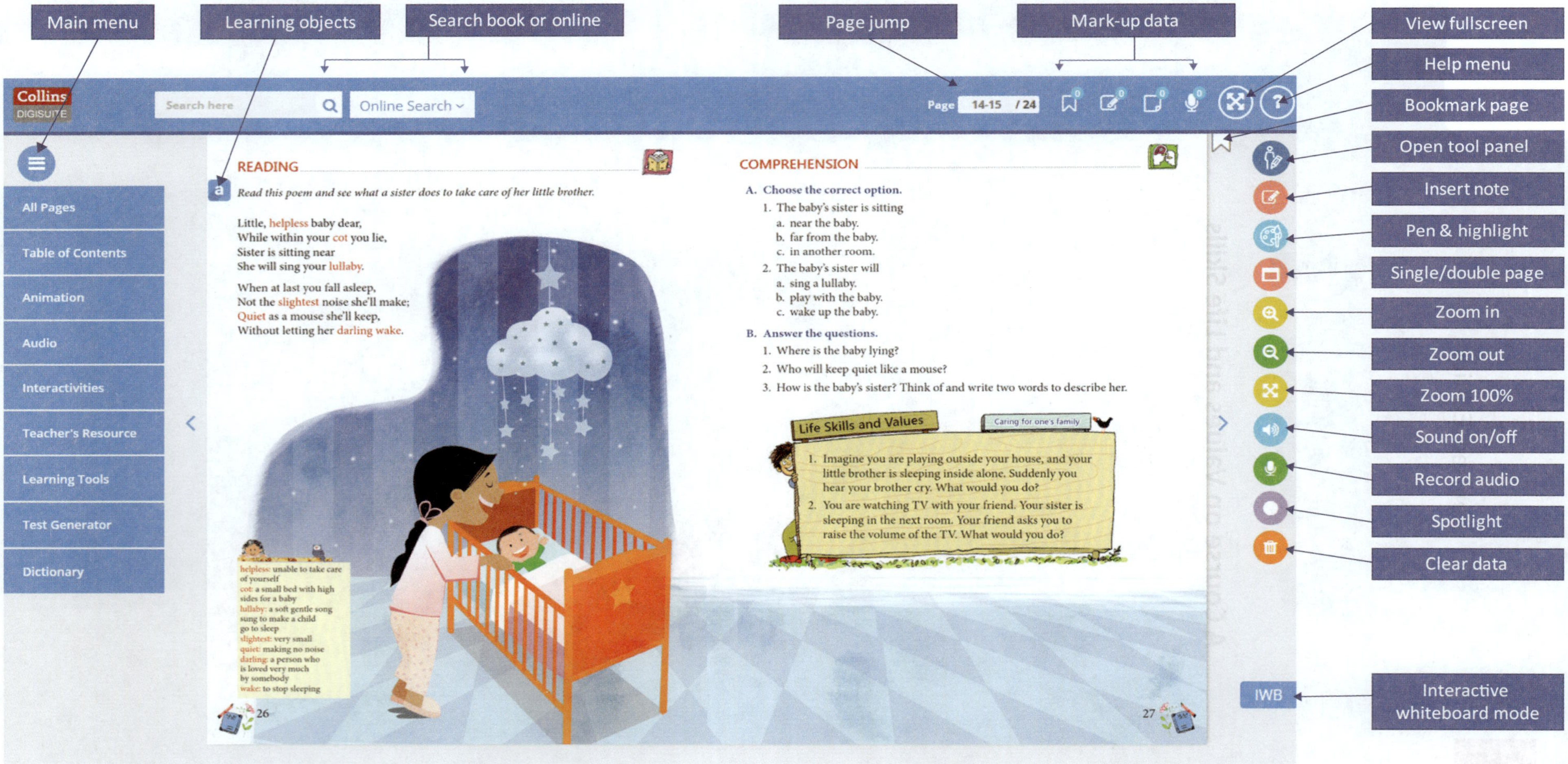
Main menu
Learning objects
Search book or online
Page jump
Mark-up data
View fullscreen
Help menu
Bookmark page
Open tool panel
Insert note
Pen & highlight
Single/double page
Zoom in
Zoom out
Zoom 100%
Sound on/off
Record audio
Spotlight
Clear data
Interactive whiteboard mode
Collins DIGISUITE
Search here
Online Search
Page 14-15 / 24
All Pages
Table of Contents
Animation
Audio
Interactivities
Teacher's Resource
Learning Tools
Test Generator
Dictionary
IWB
READING
Read this poem and see what a sister does to take care of her little brother.
Little, helpless baby dear,
While within your cot you lie,
Sister is sitting near
She will sing your lullaby.
When at last you fall asleep,
Not the slightest noise she'll make;
Quiet as a mouse she'll keep,
Without letting her darling wake.
helpless: unable to take care of yourself
cot: a small bed with high sides for a baby
lullaby: a soft gentle song sung to make a child go to sleep
slightest: very small
quiet: making no noise
darling: a person who is loved very much by somebody
wake: to stop sleeping
26
COMPREHENSION
A. Choose the correct option.
1. The baby's sister is sitting
a. near the baby.
b. far from the baby.
c. in another room.
2. The baby's sister will
a. sing a lullaby.
b. play with the baby.
c. wake up the baby.
B. Answer the questions.
1. Where is the baby lying?
2. Who will keep quiet like a mouse?
3. How is the baby's sister? Think of and write two words to describe her.
Life Skills and Values
Caring for one's family
1. Imagine you are playing outside your house, and your little brother is sleeping inside alone. Suddenly you hear your brother cry. What would you do?
2. You are watching TV with your friend. Your sister is sleeping in the next room. Your friend asks you to raise the volume of the TV. What would you do?
27

Preface

Vision Revised Edition, a course on life skills and values, is an engaging value education series meant to enable learners lead a balanced, happy and successful life. The National Education Policy, 2020 proposes the revision and revamping of all aspects of the education structure to create a new system that is aligned with the aspirational goals of 21st century education, while building upon India's traditions and value systems. It also lays focus on critical life skills and values.

Vision Revised Edition follows an interactive and multidisciplinary approach and caters to all kinds of learners with different learning styles.

Values are presented through progressively graded stories, anecdotes or poems.

Life Skills as laid down by the World Health Organization (WHO) have been covered through interesting stories.

Each book contains special chapters and colourful spreads showcasing the **United Nations Sustainable Development Goals**, which are important to achieve a just and an equitable world for all.

21st Century Skills have been mapped to each chapter with the aim of creating well-rounded individuals thriving in a constantly changing world.

Mental health and well-being of young learners is of prime importance in today's world. Therefore, **Let's Do Yoga** poster has been introduced as a brand-new feature of the book. It contains simple and doable asanas with step-by-step guidance and illustrations.

The series also focuses on mindfulness and social-emotional learning through **'happiness activities'**. Young children learn by doing, hence the series has a variety of hands-on activities, encouraging quiet reflection and sound action.

Creating a safety net for children and making them aware of **child rights** is much needed in this age and time. *Vision* Revised Edition has special advice for children through which they can face situations in which they feel afraid, pressurized or unsafe.

Vision Revised Edition comes with **Collins DigiSuite** which offers digital content packed with animated stories, slideshows and interactive activities.

***Vision* Teacher's Manuals** offer comprehensive **Lesson Plans** and **Additional Worksheets** for teachers.

In This Series ...

Vision Revised Edition adheres to the National Education Policy, 2020. Features such as 21st Century Skills, Life Skills, multiple intelligences, Sustainable Development Goals and Let's Do Yoga all align with the new policy.

Discuss

Warm-up exercise familiarizes students to the mood of the chapter

Read along

A story or a poem based on a value

Figure out

Questions based on the chapter to ensure value inculcation

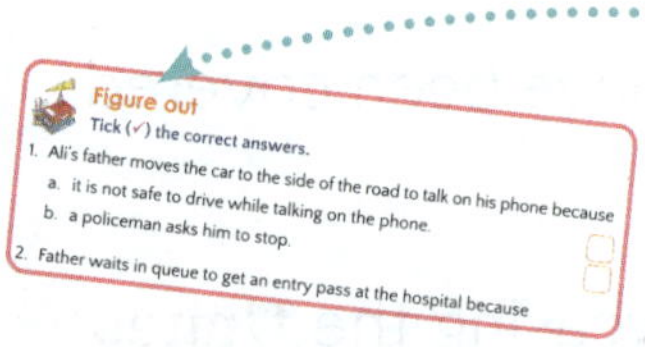

Relate

Application-based questions to check students' understanding

Project

Interesting projects based on the values taught

Happiness Activity

Interesting activities to promote 'happiness'

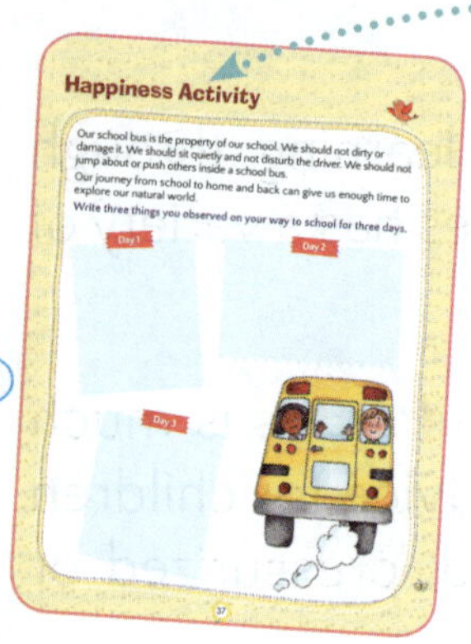

Remember

Brief pointers that the students can incorporate in their behaviour

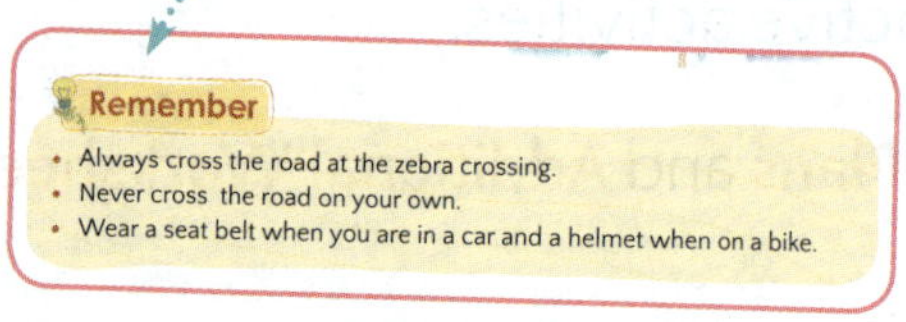

Think and Say

Thinking questions that encourage students to think laterally

Think and Say

Your best friend cannot come to your birthday party as her pet dog is sick and she is sad. How would you feel?

Happiness Box

Enjoyable activities that promote 'happiness' and exercises based on multiple intelligences addressing different learning styles

- Musical
- Interpersonal
- Visual-Spatial
- Verbal linguistic
- Naturalistic
- Intrapersonal
- Logical Mathematical
- Bodily Kinesthetic

Sustainable Development Goals

Special chapter and a colourful spread showcasing the UN Sustainable Development Goals, a set of goals aimed at changing our world for better

Poster

Colourful and interesting pull-out poster showcasing easy Yoga asanas

21st Century Skills

Skills necessary to succeed in the age of information: learning skills, literacy skills and social skills

Life Skills

Chapters focusing on WHO life skills through interesting stories

Teaching tips

- Differentiate between pride and arrogance.
- Stress on the strengths of each student.

Teaching tips

Suggestions for teachers

Detailed Contents

21st Century Skills

Learning Skills	Collaboration	Sukhi's Vacation
	Communication	Aimol Cries Wolf
	Critical Thinking	Little Sid Eats Right
Literacy Skills	Information Literacy	Ali Runs for Rules
Social Skills	Persistence	Popo Wins the Race
	Initiative	The Fish Unite
	Leadership	Proud Rex

Life Skills

Paul and the Picnic	Self-awareness
Stronger Together	Interpersonal Relationship

Projects

Project I	Make a Green Guide
Project II	The Mystery Box

Contents

1. Ali Runs for Rules

Discuss

Look at the pictures. Talk about them in class.

Read along

Ali's grandfather is not well. He is in the hospital.

Ali's father is going to visit him.

'May I come too, Father?' asks Ali.

Do you not have your football practice today?' asks Father.

'You can drop me at the football field after we meet Grandfather', says Ali.

While driving, Father's mobile starts ringing. Father moves the car to the side of the road and stops. Then, he talks on his phone.

When he finishes the call, Ali asks, 'Father, why did you stop the car to take the call?'

Father replies, 'This is a rule we follow while driving on the road. If we talk on the phone while driving, we cannot drive safely.'

When they reach the hospital, they stand in a queue to get an entry pass.

'Why can't we just go inside?' asks Ali.

Father replies, 'Because, we need to follow the rules of the hospital.'

Think and Say

It is a rule to keep wet umbrellas outside the classroom on a rainy day. One rainy morning, your teacher is not in class. What will you do with your wet umbrella?

After meeting Grandfather, Father drives Ali to the football field.

Father stops at the traffic light as it turns red.

'Father, I will be late for my practice. Please drive through', Ali requests.

'No Ali! Traffic rules are for our own safety,' says Father. 'If I drive through the red light, I will be breaking the rules of the road. If I break the rules of the road, there might be an accident,' he explains.

Ali understands that rules are very important.

He reaches the football field ten minutes late.

'Ali, you are late. Run around the field', says the football coach.

'Now Ali, do you understand why rules are important?' asks Dad, looking at Ali.

'Yes, Father!' says Ali with a smile.

He begins his run and Father smiles.

Remember

- Always cross the road at the zebra crossing.
- Never cross the road on your own.
- Wear a seat belt when you are in a car and a helmet when on a bike.

Figure out

Tick (✓) the correct answers.

1. Ali's father moves the car to the side of the road to talk on his phone because
   a. it is not safe to drive while talking on the phone. ☐
   b. a policeman asks him to stop. ☐

2. Father waits in queue to get an entry pass at the hospital because
   a. he is afraid of the hospital guard. ☐
   b. it is a hospital rule to get an entry pass to enter the hospital. ☐

3. Father stops at the traffic light because
   a. someone might get hurt if he breaks this traffic rule. ☐
   b. a traffic policeman was looking at Father. ☐

4. Ali has to run around the field because
    a. he is late for practice.
    b. he likes running.
5. Father smiles when Ali runs around the field because
    a. he wants his son to run.
    b. he knows that Ali understands that rules are important for everyone.

Relate

Draw a ☺ for the best answer.

1. You have brushed your teeth at night but you feel like eating an ice cream from the fridge. What would you do?

a. Eat the ice cream and then brush your teeth again

b. Eat the ice cream and go to bed without brushing your teeth

2. You are in the school library reading a funny book. What would you do?

a. Laugh quietly, so you do not disturb others

b. Laugh out loud

3. You finish your packet of wafers in the car. What would you do with the empty packet?

a. Throw it in a dustbin when you spot one

b. Throw it on the road

Happiness Box

1. Follow the instructions to make a Rule Placard and share it in class.

You need

- A long, strong stick
- A quarter sheet of chart paper
- Adhesive tape
- Bold markers

Steps

a. Write 'Playground Rule' on top of the paper.

b. Write any one rule that you would follow on the playground.

c. Using the adhesive tape, attach the chart paper to the stick.

d. Your Rule Placard is ready. Share your rule with the class.

2. While playing any game or sport, we need to wear the right clothes or use the right things to play. Match the sports with what we need to play them with.

Swimming
Badminton
Cycling
Football
Cricket

Teaching tips

- Give examples of parental care and talk about how students can show same care and affection towards their elders.
- Stress on unselfishness.
- Encourage students to consider the comforts of others before their own.

2. Popo Wins the Race

Discuss

Look at the pictures. Talk about them in class.

Read along

Kuru the kangaroo is the fastest runner in the forest. He wins all the races. He is proud and does not respect anyone in the forest. None of the other animals like him because of his pride.

Kuru teases Popo the penguin the most. Popo is slow and often cannot finish a race.

Mozzie the fox is in charge of the races. If animals want to race with each other, they tell Mozzie. He shows them the track they can race on.

One day, Kuru asks Popo to race with him. They go to Mozzie. Mozzie, like the other animals, wants to teach Kuru to be humble. He chooses a race track over the hill and into the lake. The race would finish on the other side of the lake.

All the animals of the forest come to see the race. 'The one who reaches the finish line first will be the winner', says Mozzie.

Mozzie counts, '3, 2, 1. Go!' and the race starts. Kuru happily climbs the hill in big leaps and jumps, into the lake. Once in the lake, Kuru struggles. He cannot swim very well.

On the other hand, Popo waddles slowly over the hill. When she reaches the lake, she jumps right in and swims to the other side of the lake in no time. Meanwhile, Kuru is still flapping his hands, legs and tail in the water. He knows how to swim, but cannot swim as fast as Popo.

At last, Kuru reaches the other bank. He is sure that Popo will make fun of him. Instead, Popo smiles and says, 'Dear Kuru, we are friends'.

Think and Say

Your best friend cannot come to your birthday party as her pet dog is sick and she is sad. How would you feel?

Mozzie adds, 'Kuru, this time Popo won the race as she is a good swimmer. You see, everybody is good at something'. Kuru is no longer so proud. He hangs his head and promises to respect everyone.

Remember

- Respect your friends.
- Say sorry when you are wrong.
- Try to know more about your friends' likes and dislikes.
- Do not behave rudely with your friends.
- Help your friends whenever you can.

Figure out

Tick (✓) the correct answers.

1. Kuru ran the fastest, so he was
   a. proud. ☐ b. humble. ☐
2. Popo was slow, but she
   a. respected Kuru. ☐ b. hated Kuru. ☐
3. Mozzie did not like
   a. Popo's pride. ☐ b. Kuru's pride. ☐

4. When Kuru reached the other side, he was sure that Popo would
   a. make fun of him. ☐ b. dance with him. ☐
5. Popo taught Kuru
   a. to respect everyone. ☐ b. to swim. ☐

Relate

Draw a 🙂 for the best answer.

1. Your friend has shared a secret with you. She asks you not to tell anybody. What would you do?

a. Tell everyone her secret ◯

b. Respect her wish and keep the secret to yourself ◯

2. Your friend's grandmother is not well. Your friend is sad and does not want to play. What would you do?

a. Respect his wish and not force him to play ◯

b. Force him to play with you ◯

3. You had a quarrel with your friend. Both of you are angry with each other. What would you do the next day?

a. Wait for her to say sorry to you ◯

b. Go to her and say sorry first ◯

Happiness Box

Birthday Card

1. Make a birthday card for any of your family members.

Materials required: Thick coloured paper, sketch pens, glue

- Take a sheet of thick paper and fold it into half.
- With the help of an adult, select a photograph of the family member and paste it on the card. You can even draw a picture.
- Draw balloons or flowers to decorate around the picture.
- Write your birthday message inside.

2. Observe your friends. Write two good things that each of them do and try to do them yourself too.

....

....

....

Teaching tips

- Differentiate between pride and arrogance.
- Stress on the strengths of each student.

3. Holly Loves Lavender

Discuss

Look at the pictures. Talk about them in class.

Read along

Life on earth consists of many animals and plants and other life forms linked to each other. Therefore, it is important that we protect them. The global goal, Life on Land, encourages and looks for ways to protect the animals and plants on land.

15 LIFE ON LAND

Holly was a rabbit who loved lavender. She loved its smell, its taste and even its colour. Wherever she found lavender, she would start munching it. Holly ate so much lavender that she became really big. Soon, she was the biggest rabbit in the burrow. Yet, she could not stop eating lavender.

The other rabbits in the burrow began to worry. Lavender was vanishing from their gardens. Holly ate it all. Lavender was not just food for the rabbits. Lavender was a herb. It was medicine to cure sick rabbits, too.

Soon, some rabbits from the burrow fell sick. There was no lavender to cure them. What would happen now?

Holly became sad. She had been greedy and eaten up all the lavender. She did not think that it would take so much time for the lavender plants to grow back.

One day, Holly saw a small sprig of lavender in the forest. She had not eaten any lavender for weeks. She wanted so much to bite into the sweet smelling leaves. She remembered the rabbits who were ill. She carefully cleared the ground around the tiny plant and watered it. Every day she cared for it. Soon it grew tall and other tiny lavender plants started growing around it.

Think and Say

You notice that your younger sister does not switch off the lights of the room when she leaves. What would you do?

When the rabbits got to know, they thanked Holly. They took a few leaves from each plant and fed them to the sick rabbits. Holly was happy, she could help others.

Remember

- All plants and animals are our friends.
- Never hurt plants or animals.
- Never pluck flowers or tear leaves.
- Do not waste paper. Paper comes from trees and wasting paper means killing trees
- If you see an open tap, turn it off.

Figure out

Tick (✓) the correct answers.

1. Do you think it was right for Holly to eat all the lavender?
   a. Yes, because she liked it. ☐
   b. No, because she did not leave any for others. ☐

2. What happened when there was no more lavender left for the other rabbits?
   a. They could not be cured when they fell ill. ☐
   b. They were happy. ☐

3. Holly took care of the lavender plant she found. Why do you think she did this?
   a. Holly felt sad about her actions in the past and wanted to make things right. ☐
   b. She wanted to eat more lavender. ☐

4. If Holly knew what her actions would lead to, would she have eaten all the lavender?
   a. Yes ☐ b. No ☐

5. Do you think that Holly will eat all the lavender ever again?

   a. Yes, because it is tasty.

   b. No, because she has seen what the result can be.

Relate

Draw a 🙂 for the best answer.

1. If you see a man cutting a tree in your backyard, what would you do?

a. Let him cut it down

b. Ask elders to tell them to stop

2. If you saw a baby plant growing in your garden, what would you do?

a. Water it to help the plant grow

b. Not care whether it grew or not

3. If you heard a hungry kitten outside your home, what would you do?

a. Leave the kitten alone

b. Give the kitten some food

Happiness Box

1. **Wrapping Sheet**

   Things required: A thin chart paper, ladies' fingers, colours

   - Take a thin chart paper.
   - Take one ladies' fingers and cut one end of it.
   - Dip it in paint and make prints on the chart paper.
   - Use the paper to wrap gifts.

2. **What is Living Up on the Trees?**

   Walk around your neighbourhood, with a pair of binoculars if possible.

   - What do you see just above the ground in the bushes? What is living up on the trees? You might see leaves, insects, mushrooms and plants.
   - How do these creatures get up onto the branch?
   - How do these creatures interact with each other to find food and shelter?
   - Be careful while you work, wear gloves if necessary! Make a short report and share it in class.

Teaching tips

- Bring out the unexpected dangers of Holly's actions.
- Tell children about how electricity and environment are connected.
- Talk to the children about the environment in totality, that is, oceans, underground environment, forest and space.

4. Sukhi's Vacation

Discuss

Look at the pictures. Talk about them in class.

Read along

Sukhi was visiting her grandfather during the vacation. Her grandfather is a farmer.

Grandfather and Sukhi would get up very early. They had many things to do on the farm. Grandfather would milk the cow. Sukhi would gather the eggs from the coop. Grandfather would cook breakfast. Sukhi would feed hay to the cows and grains to the hens.

Then Sukhi would go to play and Grandfather would go to the fields. When Grandfather returned, they would have lunch. After some rest, both of them would go around the farm again. They had to see that the animals were resting.

Think and Say

You see that your father is washing the car. What would you do?

At night, Grandfather would tell Sukhi stories till they both fell asleep.

One morning, Grandfather fell ill. When Sukhi saw that he was not feeling well, she tucked him in his bed. She said, 'Grandfather, please rest. Today, I will take care of your chores and all the animals'.

Grandfather groaned, That is a lot of work, Sukhi. You will not be able to manage all this on your own'.

Sukhi shook her head. 'Grandfather, you cared for me. You always looked after me when I was sick. Now it is my turn', she said patting his hand.

Grandfather smiled and laid back on his pillows.

Sukhi ran around the farm doing everything she could. She also took care of Grandfather. She fed him hot soup. By that evening, Grandfather felt better.

Grandfather said, 'Sukhi, you have helped me so much'. Sukhi just smiled and asked him to rest.

Later, Grandfather told everyone, 'My Sukhi is the best granddaughter I could ever have'.

—Sutapa Basu

Remember

- Helping people is rewarding.
- We can make others happy by helping them.
- Always look for ways in which we can help someone in need.
- Small good deeds matter a lot.

Figure out

Tick (✓) the correct answers.

1. Why did Sukhi run around the farm doing everything she could?
   a. Because Sukhi hated to work on the farm. ☐
   b. Because Sukhi had a lot of work to complete and she had to take care of Grandfather as well. ☐

2. Should Grandfather have forced himself to get up and do the work?
   a. Yes, he was not too ill. ☐
   b. No, it is better to take rest when you are ill so that you recover quickly. ☐

3. Should Sukhi have left the work of the farm for the next day?
   a. No, Sukhi did the right thing by helping her Grandfather. ☐
   b. Yes, it is all right for work to be left for the next day. ☐

4. Do you think Sukhi should have been rewarded for helping Grandfather?
   a. Yes, after all, she did extra work. ☐
   b. No, helping others is a selfless act. ☐

5. Do you think Sukhi is the best granddaughter?

   a. Yes ☐

   b. No ☐

Relate

Draw a 🙂 for the best answer.

1. Your friend missed school because she was ill, and a test is coming up, what would you do?

a. Let her be as she is

b. Help her study for the test

2. A blind man is walking on the pavement. He is about to walk into a lamp post. What would you do?

a. Let him walk on

b. Help him immediately

3. You see a book drop out of a person's bag. Unaware, she walks on. What would you do?

a. Pick up the book and give it to her

b. Let the book be where it is

Happiness Box

1. Make cards for three people who helped you in the past week. Decorate them and write 'Thank you for your help' on them. Inside the card, write a short note to the person.
2. Match the following helpful actions with the pictures.

Helping a friend with the lessons he missed because he was unwell.

Helping your mother and father lay the table.

Helping a friend carry his bag.

Helping your younger sister clean her cupboard.

Teaching tips

- Stress on how personalities like Mother Teresa helped others selflessly.
- Tell students that when they help someone in need without expecting anything in return, it is a selfless act.
- Tell students about the circle of help—that help always comes back twofold when least expected, but most needed.

5. Paul and the Picnic

Discuss

Look at the pictures. Talk about them in class.

Read along

Paul woke up late every day. He took a lot of time to bathe and dress and was always late to the breakfast table. He would never reach school on time. His teacher scolded him for being late but Paul did not care.

One day, Paul's teacher told the class that they were to go for a school picnic the next day. Paul was very excited. He loved picnics. Paul's teacher told everyone to reach the school at 8:00 a.m. The bus would leave exactly at 8:15 a.m. Knowing that Paul was always late, his teacher told him, especially, to be punctual.

Think and Say

Your alarm clock has stopped working. How can you still wake up on time?

Paul asked his mother to wake him on time. Next morning, his mother woke him. As usual, he did not get up and was late. Even though his father dropped him to school, he reached only at 8:20 a.m. By then, the bus had left with all his classmates and there was nobody in his class.

Paul was very sad. He returned home crying. His mother made him sit on her lap. She wiped his tears and then spoke to him gently. 'Paul, this has happened because you have made it a habit to be late. What do you think you should do?' She asked.

'Mother, I know it is my fault. I promise you and myself that I will never be late again,' he said.

From that day onwards, Paul got up early every morning. He was never late for school again.

Remember

- Wake up early.
- Plan a daily timetable and follow it.
- Pack your bag according to the class timetable before going to bed.
- Keep your school uniform on a hanger with shoes and socks ready before going to bed.
- Set your clock ahead of time by 10 minutes. This will help you to be on time.

Figure out

Tick (✓) the correct answers.

1. When Paul woke up late

   a. he reached school late and was scolded by his teachers. ☐

   b. he could not attend school. ☐

2. Paul missed the picnic because

   a. he could not reach school on time. ☐

   b. he did not want to go for the picnic. ☐

3. Paul was sad because

   a. he did not do well in his subjects. ☐

   b. he missed the picnic. ☐

4. What did Paul realize?

   a. He realized that he should make it a habit to be on time. ☐

   b. He realized that missing lessons is a good habit. ☐

5. At the end, Paul changed his habit. Write four good things that would have happened to Paul had he always been on time.

   a. ....

   b. ....

   c. ....

   d. ....

Relate

Draw a 🙂 for the best answer.

1. Your friend and you are supposed to go for a birthday party. Your friend is late. What would you do?

a. Get angry and shout at him

b. Help him understand why it is important to be on time

2. Your friend misses classes because he is late and asks for your notebook to take down the notes. What would you do?

a. Not give him the notebook

b. Give him the notebook and ask him not to be late again

3. You are late for a movie with your friends and everybody misses the movie. Your friends get angry. What would you do?

a. Ignore my friends

b. Say sorry to my friends

Happiness Box

1. **It is important to follow a timetable. Make your daily routine and hang it in your room.**

You need

- Coloured chart paper
- Scissors
- Coloured markers
- Ribbon
- Compass

Steps

- Draw a big circle on the chart paper and cut it out.
- Write the time and the activity that you do in that time slot in the different parts of the circle.
- Decorate it as you like.
- Fold the ribbon in a loop and paste it at the back of the circle.

2. **Arrange these ten words related to time in alphabetical order.**

second	hour	calendar	clock	year
minute	day	month	week	time

Teaching tips

- Tell students how being late affects the schedule of other people.
- Stress on how many people have to be on time so that students can attend classes.
- Talk about how parents have to leave for work or get up on time.
- Give examples of activities and people who follow a timetable for work.

Happiness Activity

Our school bus is the property of our school. We should not dirty or damage it. We should sit quietly and not disturb the driver. We should not jump about or push others inside a school bus.

Our journey from school to home and back can give us enough time to explore our natural world.

Write three things you observed on your way to school for three days.

Day 1

Day 2

Day 3

Colour the picture. Circle the actions we should not do on a school bus.

Project I : Make a Green Guide

Look around your neighbourhood. Are there any places where you can find different plants and smell the scents of flowers? Make a list of all such places. You can include places like parks, flower shops, plant nurseries and so on. Draw a picture of each place and write two or three sentences about what you have seen there. Share your guide in class.

6. Aimol Cries Wolf

Discuss

Look at the pictures. Talk about them in class.

Read along

Little Aimol loved playing pranks.

He would tease everyone and play pranks on them. He would also lie to his family. He would scare his sister by saying, 'Look at the rats under your bed! They will bite you at night'. His sister would get scared and cry.

One day, his grandmother was boiling soup. Aimol took a spoonful and said, 'Yuck! No salt.' His grandmother mixed some more salt into it though she had, in fact, put salt in it earlier. That evening, nobody could have the salty soup!

Think and Say

Your friend is asking you to play a prank on another friend. What would you do?

Another day, he told his father, 'Dad, your car has been stolen!' His dad ran out instantly. The car was found right in the middle of their driveway. Inside the house, Aimol was rolling on the carpet, laughing so hard that his stomach hurt.

One night, Grandfather decided to tell him the story of the shepherd boy who played a prank by shouting, 'Wolf! Wolf!'

'So, when the wolf really came, and the boy shouted 'wolf', nobody believed him', said Grandfather. Aimol only laughed when Grandfather finished the story and went off to sleep.

That night, something strange happened. Aimol heard some screeching noises and woke up with a startle. It was dark. The noises were coming from under his bed. He peeped and was horrified! There were rats and rats and rats under his bed. He shouted, 'Mum! Dad! Rats! Rats!' But, nobody came.

Aimol jumped from his bed and ran to the living room. Everyone sat there, chatting. He said, 'Come quickly! There are rats under my bed!' Nobody even looked at him. Aimol shouted again, 'I am not lying. Please believe me!' Nobody even bothered to get up.

'Aimol! Aimol!' called someone. Aimol opened his eyes. It was Grandfather.

Aimol sat up. 'The rats?' he said.

'What rats?' his grandfather asked, 'You were shouting in your sleep. Did you have a bad dream?'

'So all those rats were a dream!' Aimol sighed with relief. From that day, Aimol decided never to tell lies again. Never did he play pranks on anyone to trouble them either.

Remember

- Lying is a bad habit.
- When we lie, we hurt people.
- If you always lie, no one will believe you when you speak the truth.
- Being truthful is a good quality. We must practise it.

Figure out

Tick (✓) the correct answers.

1. Do you think scaring someone as a prank is fun?
   a. Yes, it is fun. ☐
   b. No, it is not fun. ☐
2. Do you think Aimol could have found a better way to spend his time?
   a. No, playing pranks is a good hobby. ☐
   b. Yes, Aimol could have spent his time more wisely by reading, painting or learning to play an instrument. ☐
3. Do you think that Aimol's dream actually taught him a lesson?
   a. Yes, Aimol needed to realize that lying is bad. ☐
   b. No, Aimol continued to play pranks. ☐
4. Do you think Grandfather told the story of the boy who cried 'Wolf!' to Aimol on purpose?
   a. Yes, so that Aimol could learn from the story. ☐
   b. No, he just told him a story. ☐
5. Do you think Aimol will play more pranks in future?
   a. Yes, I think so. ☐
   b. No, I do not think so. ☐

Relate

Draw a for the best answer.

1. While playing cricket, the ball you hit broke your car's windscreen. What would you do?

a. Tell an elder that you broke it

b. Lie about it

2. Last night, you were sleepy and could not finish your homework. What would you tell your teacher?

a. Lie to your teacher and tell her that you were ill

b. Tell your teacher the truth

3. You have broken your brother's toy. What would you do?

a. Tell him that you broke his toy and say sorry

b. Hide the broken toy

Happiness Box

1. Collect coloured paper or chart paper from your home or school. Make bookmarks using them. With the help of your teacher cut them neatly in the shape of a bookmark. Colour them and write the word HONESTY on them. Share the bookmarks with your classmates.

2. Write two words that mean the opposite of the words 'lie' and 'truth'.

....

....

....

....

Teaching tips

- Tell students about the concepts of honesty and dishonesty and include examples such as cheating and bribing.
- Stress on ways to make better use of time, such as working on a hobby.
- Tell students about the rewards of being honest and consequences of being dishonest.
- Tell them that we are responsible for the results of our actions.

7. The Fish Unite

Discuss

Look at the pictures. Talk about them in class.

Read along

Deep in the forest was a big river. All kinds of fish lived in the river. Each group of fish was different. No group was friendly with the other group.

All the groups lived and played separately. The elder fish kept telling the younger fish to remain together and united. The younger fish did not listen to them.

One day, a big fish, named Sim, came into the river. She started eating the small fish one by one. Every day some fish from each group went missing.

'What is happening? Why are our numbers decreasing every day?' asked a fish one day.

'I think Sim is eating our brothers and sisters,' replied another fish.

Concerned, all the groups of fish went to their elders.

'Please help us or Sim will eat us all up', said one small fish.

'This was the reason we had told you to be united', said the elder fish.

'Now listen carefully and do as we say', said another elder.

The younger fish listened carefully and understood the plan.

The next day when Sim came to eat the small fish, she saw a much bigger fish than herself. All the small fish groups had united to make one fish. Swimming together, they looked like a very big fish.

Sim was very frightened. She swam fast for her life as the large fish chased her. She left the river as fast as she could and never came back again.

'Hurray!' the younger fish cheered.

Think and Say

Your mother is not well today. How can your brother and you work together to care for your mother?

They celebrated their unity.

'Now do you see how unity helps? When all of you unite to face danger, you win', said the elders.

'Oh yes! From now on, we will always remain united', said all the younger fish.

Remember

- In school, you can have unity by taking part in all activities.
- You can have unity at home by helping with the housework.
- You can have unity with your friends by playing a game that everyone likes.

Figure out

Tick (✓) the correct answers.

1. The different groups of fish living in the river were
   a. friendly with each other. ☐ b. unfriendly with each other. ☐

2. The elder fish asked the younger fish to
   a. remain united.
   b. fight among themselves.
3. Sim was able to eat the small fish because
   a. they were naughty.
   b. they were not united.
4. To get rid of Sim, all the small fish
   a. united together.
   b. left the stream.
5. Sim swam away because
   a. she was a coward.
   b. the small fish had united.

Relate

Draw a 🙂 for the best answer.

1. A few students of your class are selected for the annual play competition. What should the others do?

a. Unite and help them prepare for it

b. Stop talking to them

2. Your friend's bicycle is stuck in the mud. What would you do?

a. Leave him there

b. Help him to take the cycle out

3. Some older boys ask you to leave the park for them to play. What would you do?

a. Quietly leave the park

b. Get together and discuss how both the groups can play

Happiness Box

1. **Make Family T-shirts for Your Cousins**

You need

- A coloured t-shirt for each cousin
- Fabric paint

Steps

- Take the t-shirt.
- With the help of an adult, write the name of the team on the t-shirt.
- Decorate the t-shirt using fabric colours.

You can wear this t-shirt at the next family get together and also gift these to your other cousins.

2. **Good communication is important for unity in a team. Form two groups in class with a leader for each. In this activity, you must make a structure using building blocks.**

The teacher will show the team leader a house made of building blocks but will not tell him or her how the blocks were put together.

- Look at the structure carefully and then go to other team members and describe the structure to them.
- The team should try to make the structure again, helping each other.
- If they get it wrong, the team leader must try again till they get it right.

Teaching tips

- Stress on the need to stay united in class.
- Give more examples of unity from life.
- Make students aware of the difference between right and wrong.

8. Stronger Together

Discuss

Look at the pictures. Talk about them in class.

Read along

One day, our teacher, Renu Ma'am divided the drama class into groups. There were three children in each group. She wanted each group to enact a play.

Radha, Azim and Jassi were in one group.

'I cannot act', said Jassi.

'Neither can I', said Azim.

'That is okay, I can act', Radha volunteered.

How will we do the play together?' Radha asked.

Azim had an idea. Let us put up a puppet show. He told Jassi, 'Jassi, you are good at art and craft. Can you make the puppets? I am good at games, so I will take care of the puppet show'.

I am good at acting, so I will say the dialogues,' Radha added.

'Wow! This sounds great!' Jassi said happily.

All the three started doing what they were good at.

In no time, Jassi made the puppets, Radha wrote and rehearsed her dialogues, while Azim planned out the show.

When it was time for them to perform, everything was ready and in place. With Jassi's puppets, Radha's dialogues and Azim's planning, the three friends put up a great puppet show.

Think and Say

Your father wants to take you and your friend for a movie. Your friend falls sick. What would you do?

As their play ended, Renu Ma'am clapped and said, 'I am very happy with this group's play. Each student did what he or she is good at and made the play a success. This is real cooperation. Jassi, Azim and Radha are the winners'.

All the students clapped, while Radha, Jassi and Azim stood together and beamed with happiness.

Remember

- You can cooperate with friends by sharing responsibilities.
- Cooperation does not mean that you do your friend's homework.
- Sometimes, play games that your friends like, instead of games that you like.

Figure out

Tick (✓) the correct answers.

1. The drama class was divided into groups of
   a. three children. ☐ b. two children. ☐
2. Radha, Jassi and Azim's group presented a
   a. dance show. ☐ b. puppet show. ☐
3. Radha, Jassi and Azim decided to
   a. cooperate with each other. ☐ b. give up putting up a play. ☐
4. The three children worked as a team. Each one did what they were
   a. good at. ☐ b. not good at. ☐
5. Radha, Jassi and Azim were winners because
   a. they cooperated with each other. ☐
   b. they fought with each other. ☐

Relate

Draw a ☺ for the best answer.

1. Your friend and you have to make a picture chart for the class together. What would you do?

a. Divide the work and complete the project

b. Fight with your friend

2. You have come to play with your cousin, but she has to finish making her scrapbook. What would you do?

a. Help her make the scrapbook

b. Not help her and complain of being bored

3. The children in your class are participating in a pyramid competition. What would you do?

a. Not participate in the competition

b. Enjoy participating in the competition

Happiness Box

1. Firefighters, cricketers and footballers need to work as a team in order to get their jobs done. Think of some other types of jobs that need a group of people to work together. Write these down on a coloured chart paper. Write three ways in which each member helps the team.

2. **Play this game in groups of four.**

Ball on the Blanket

a. Each group is given a blanket.

b. Each person will hold one corner of the blanket.

c. Place a ball in the centre of the blanket.

d. On the 'GO' signal, you have to push together to throw the ball off the blanket and into the air.

e. Then, you have to catch the ball on its way down.

f. The team that makes the maximum number of bounces and catches, within a particular time, wins the game.

3. **Write the first letters of these phrases to get a new word.**

Write the new word and discuss what this word means to you?

....

Get along

Respect others

Obey rules

Use low voices

Participate

Teaching tips

- Make students aware of the importance of working in teams.
- Tell them that trusting others is important for teamwork.
- Tell students about how teams are built around individual strengths.

9. Proud Rex

Discuss

Look at the pictures. Talk about them in class.

Read along

Once in a forest, there lived a group of crows. One crow among them was stronger than the rest. His name was Rex.

Rex could fly higher and faster than all the crows. He always boasted that he knew one hundred and one ways of flying. The other crows were very impressed and made him their king. Soon, he became King Rex, an arrogant bird.

One day, from a land far away, an eagle came to the forest. His name was Aquila. The crows saw Aquila flying in the sky. They were impressed by the manner in which he was flying. When he landed, they gathered around him.

They boasted about King Rex to Aquila. One crow said, 'Our king is the greatest.'

Another crow said, 'Yes, he knows a lot of different ways of flying. He is truly great!' The other crows then cawed loudly cheering Rex.

Although Aquila was simple and wise, he was quite taken aback by the crows' praise of their king. Hearing about the glory of King Rex, Aquila expressed his wish to meet him. He asked, 'May I have the honour of meeting King Rex?'

The crows happily led him to meet King Rex. Aquila bowed low before King Rex and said, 'I am grateful to have met you, O great king!'

The king asked, 'How many ways can you fly?'

The wise Aquila was surprised. He said, 'I know only one way to fly, O king!'

King Rex puffed his chest and said, 'I know one hundred and one ways of flying. Let me show you some.' Then he went on to show Aquila his acrobatic flying.

Think and Say
Would you admit in class that you do not know an answer?

Finally, when King Rex landed, he said, 'Now Aquila, you show me your way.'

Eagles fly very high and very fast. So Aquila rose slowly and easily into the sky. King Rex went along too. Then Aquila gained speed and flew even higher. Soon he was soaring in the sky and flying very, very fast. King Rex was only a crow. He could not keep up with the skill of an eagle. As he struggled to fly alongside Aquila, he fell into the sea.

The arrogant king was about to drown. In the nick of time, Aquila dived down and saved King Rex. He picked up King Rex with his strong claws and took him back to the forest.

As King Rex recovered, he realized his foolishness. Humbled by Aquila's skill and modesty, King Rex was never arrogant about his flying again. Soon, the modest Aquila and the humbled king became good friends.

Remember

- Be humble.
- Be happy with the little joys of life.
- Share your things.
- Do not show off what you have.
- Do not compare yourself with others.
- Do not demand things that others have.

Figure out

Tick (✓) the correct answers.

1. Why do you think the other crows made Rex their king?
   a. They were impressed by how strong Rex was. ☐
   b. They were scared of how strong Rex was. ☐

2. Why do you think King Rex was foolish?
   a. He was proud of something that did not make him a better king. ☐
   b. He had to take help from Aquila. ☐

3. How do you know that Aquila was simple and wise?
   a. Aquila did not show off even though he was a better flyer. ☐
   b. Aquila also thought that the crow should be the king. ☐

4. What led to King Rex's downfall?
   a. His pride and that he showed off. ☐
   b. His simplicity. ☐

5. Could King Rex's one hundred and one ways of flying help him in any way?

   a. Yes ☐

   b. No ☐

Relate

Draw a 🙂 for the best answer.

1. If someone tries to put you down by showing off their latest video game, what would you do?

a. Listen quietly and not show off in return ◯

b. Ask your father to get one so that you can show off too ◯

2. Your neighbour has bought a new cricket set and shows it off. How would you feel?

a. Jealous ◯

b. Happy for him ◯

3. Your father has got you a new bicycle. Which of these would you do?

a. Brag about it to all my friends ◯

b. Allow my friends to ride it too ◯

Happiness Box

1. **Make a poster of this poem. Decorate it with colourful pictures and share it in the class.**

Little Things

Little drops of water,
Little grains of sand,
Make the mighty ocean,
And the pleasant land.
Thus the little minutes,
Humble though they be,
Make the mighty ages,
Of eternity.

—Ebenezer Cobham Brewer

2. **What do you see in the picture below? Write in the space provided.**

....
....
....
....
....
....
....
....

Teaching tips

- Talk about the concept of humility.
- Stress on the difference between humility and low self-esteem.
- Ask students to give examples of humility from daily life.

10. Little Sid Eats Right

Discuss

Look at the pictures. Talk about them in class.

Read along

Sid did not want to wake up on the first day of his holidays. He had to go with his parents to visit his grandparents at their farm for a week. Sid loved his grandparents dearly, but he would not get his favourite potato chips outside the city. How could he live without chips! So, in his tiny bag, Sid filled packets and packets of his favourite chips.

At the farm, he greeted his grandmother, grandfather and their dog, Scrappy. While his parents and grandparents chatted, Sid quietly went out of the room. Carefully, he took a handful of chips from his bag and gobbled them up. Then, he ran out to play.

Sid munched chips all through the day. So, he was never hungry at mealtimes. He said no to porridge, no to milk, no to carrots and no to beans.

Something else also happened. He felt tired all the time. If he ran with Scrappy, he became breathless and wanted to sit down.

After two days of gobbling chips, Sid had no more chips. What would he eat now!

'Chips are junk food, Sid. How long will you not eat real food?' Grandfather said.

Finally, his grandmother said, 'Search for potatoes in the vegetable patch, Sid. If you find any, I will make chips for you.' Sid happily picked up a large basket and went to the vegetable patch.

Sid searched and searched but found no potatoes. Tired and sulky, he walked into Grandmother's kitchen with a basket full of carrots and a cabbage.

Think and Say

Some people fall sick more often than others. This is because some people are weaker than others. The ability of our body to fight an illness is called immunity. Some foods help us stay strong and get well fast. Say names of one fruit and one vegetable that build our immunity.

At dinner, Sid saw some green leaves on a plate, an orange jelly in a bowl, a cool orange juice, orange chips and some warm orange drink in another bowl.

Sid wanted to know what they were. Grandmother said, 'The green leaves are fried cabbage. The orange jelly is carrot halwa, the orange juice is carrot juice, the orange chips are, of course, carrot chips and the warm orange drink in the bowl is a carrot and cabbage soup.'

One by one, Sid tasted each. His mouth started curling into a wide grin. He could not believe that carrots and cabbage tasted even better than chips!

He had carrots and cabbage for the rest of the week. He was never tired again.

Remember

We must eat healthy food because:

- it gives us energy.
- it does not let us fall ill.
- it builds our bones and muscles.
- it repairs our bodies when we fall ill.

We must eat very little junk food because:

- it does not give us any of the things that healthy food gives us.
- it can make us sick.

Figure out

Tick (✓) the correct answers.

1. Sid did not want to go to his grandparents' farm because
   a. he did not like them. ☐
   b. he would not get his favourite brand of chips there. ☐
2. Sid did not eat at mealtimes because
   a. he had eaten chips and was not hungry. ☐
   b. his grandmother had scolded him. ☐
3. Sid felt tired because
   a. he ate chips all the time. ☐
   b. he was sick. ☐
4. Sid happily went to the vegetable patch
   a. to search for potatoes. ☐ b. to search for carrots. ☐
5. When Sid ate carrots and cabbages every day, he felt
   a. happy and active. ☐ b. tired and breathless. ☐

Relate

Draw a 🙂 for the best answer.

1. You have got cucumber sandwiches for your school break. You do not like them. What would you do?

a. Eat the sandwiches as they are healthy

b. Buy a burger from the school canteen as it is tastier

2. At a school fair, you have ten rupees to buy a snack. What will you buy?

a. Mixed vegetable pulao

b. Chips and cola

3. You want to call your friends home for lunch. Your mother says she will cook a meal for your friends. What will you say to your mother?

a. You will thank her for the meal for your friends

b. You will say that you want to order pizzas for your friends

Happiness Box

1. **Follow these steps to make a delicious cucumber sandwich.**

You need

- Two slices of bread
- Butter
- Four cucumber slices

Steps

- Keep the two slices of bread on a plate.
- Spread butter on both the slices.
- Place the cucumber slices on one bread slice.
- Cover it with the other slice and press down.
- Your delicious cucumber sandwich is ready.

2. **Make your daily food chart for a five days. Write what you ate for lunch, dinner and breakfast.**

	Day 1	Day 2	Day 3	Day 4	Day 5
Lunch					
Dinner					
Breakfast					

3. Can you guess the names of these fruits and vegetables?

1. Which vegetable comes in layers and can make you cry?
2. Which fruit is the same colour as its name?
3. Which vegetable grows under the ground and has eyes?
4. Which summer fruit is big and green outside and red and juicy inside?
5. Which juicy fruit can be eaten whole and in slices, drunk as a juice and cooked into pickles and chutneys?

Teaching tips

- Tell students about different foods that give us energy, heal our body build bones and muscles.
- You may draw the food pyramid which the children would be learning in EVS or Science.
- Talk about food that can become tasty when cooked in certain ways.
- Stress on eating more healthy food and less junk food.

Goal 2: Zero Hunger

One in nine people go to bed hungry every day.

Two in ten children under the age of five are not healthy enough.

Some children have plenty of food, while others do not have enough to eat.

People go hungry because:

- they do not have money to buy food.
- crops get destroyed due to bad climate.
- farmers are not able to buy fertilizers to increase produce.

Take A Stand!

Donate food that you cannot eat to the needy

Distribute food amongst children from poor families

Never waste food

People with enough means should help those with very less means during difficult times

Project II : The Mystery Box

Form two teams of three each. Name the teams A and B.

Take an old shoe box with a lid. This can be the mystery box.

1. Groups A and B should stand facing each other and place the mystery box in the centre.
2. Group A places a few things in the box such that Group B cannot see them.
3. Let one person from Group A describe a thing that has been placed in the box by describing it. The person has to be careful not to say the name of the thing. A person from Group B should guess the name of the thing. For example, for a toy plane, one can say:

   It flies in the sky. We can go from one place to another in it.

Continue playing the game till everyone had has a chance to play. Only three hints are allowed per try. If someone cannot guess the object in three hints, it means he or she needs to work on cooperating and try again later.

At the end, judge how many pairs could cooperate well to complete the task.